NEW EDITION

Everyone Wins!

Everyone Wins!

Cooperative Games and Activities

Josette & Ba Luvmour

NEW SOCIETY PUBLISHERS

Cataloging in Publication Data:
A catalog record for this publication is available from the National Library of Canada.

First edition copyright © 1990 by Josette and Sambhava Luvmour.
Updated edition copyright © 2007 by Josette and Sambhava Luvmour.
All rights reserved.

Cover design by Diane McIntosh. Photos: Getty Images
Interior layout: Mary Jane Jessen

Printed in Canada.
First printing January 2007.

Paperback ISBN- 978-0-86571-587-5

Inquiries regarding requests to reprint all or part of *Everyone Wins!* should be addressed to New Society Publishers at the address below.

To order directly from the publishers, please call toll-free (North America) 1-800-567-6772, or order online at www.newsociety.com

Any other inquiries can be directed by mail to:

New Society Publishers
P.O. Box 189, Gabriola Island, BC V0R 1X0, Canada
1-800-567-6772

New Society Publishers' mission is to publish books that contribute in fundamental ways to building an ecologically sustainable and just society, and to do so with the least possible impact on the environment, in a manner that models this vision. We are committed to doing this not just through education, but through action. We are acting on our commitment to the world's remaining ancient forests by phasing out our paper supply from ancient forests worldwide. This book is one step toward ending global deforestation and climate change. It is printed on acid-free paper that is **100% old growth forest-free** (100% post-consumer recycled), processed chlorine free, and printed with vegetable-based, low-VOC inks. For further information, or to browse our full list of books and purchase securely, visit our website at: www.newsociety.com

NEW SOCIETY PUBLISHERS www.newsociety.com

To Amber

For the Spirit in which
she comes to play

Contents

Activity Level Two

Activity Level Three

Activity Level Four

Activity Level Five

Introduction to the First Edition

THERE WAS BIG TROUBLE ON THE PLAYGROUND at the local Waldorf School. Violence was present almost every day, and most of the first and second grade children had formed cliques. The parent who had the responsibility for monitoring the playground was getting angrier and angrier and lacked support for coping with the situation. The teachers acknowledged the problem, and saw it as an extension of difficulties in the classroom, but their every attempt to help backfired. The parents blamed other parents and other children for the problem, and the administration and other teachers were growing increasingly alarmed. It was at this point that we were called in. Was there any way to relieve the pressure short of major surgery?

Since this is an introduction to cooperative games and activities, we won't describe in detail the different means used to ease the tensions at this school. Cooperative games and activities weren't sufficient unto themselves, but they were the critical factor. They not only provided a common ground for all to meet upon, but allowed us to test the effectiveness of the other conflict resolution techniques being employed. The games served both diagnostic and remedial purposes.

The first time we met the class on the playground we had them play "Spaghetti." This was our way of saying to them that we are all interconnected and, though sometimes relationships become knotted up, it is possible to find a solution. "Spaghetti" is played by having everyone stand in a circle, then each person taking the hand of someone not directly next to them. Each person must be holding the hand of two different people. The object is to recreate the circle while continuing to hold hands. This is not easy to do, and there is often no way to do it, but communication and patience are emphasized if there is to be any chance at all. Once children get the idea they want very much to have success. This class played twice, with manners no one would have believed possible, before finally "winning."

Next, we played "Rolling Along." In this game, children pair off, lie on their backs and have to roll down a field with their toes connected. At first we let them pick their own partners, then we chose partners randomly, and finally we deliberately matched certain students together. Of course there was dissatisfaction with both the random and deliberate methods of pairing, but the game was so much fun, and the release of energy so significant that the children cooperated.

Then, it was into group games such as "Chase in the Ocean" and "True or False." Then we collectively made an obstacle course, and collectively navigated it. Finally, we played "Hug a Tree." This was an important moment in the day, for this game requires a high degree of trust. Children are in pairs and one is blindfolded. Then, in a fairly dense wood, the sighted child leads the blindfolded partner to a tree by a circuitous route. The blindfolded child explores the tree with all senses but sight. Then, via a different route, the child is led back to start, the blindfold removed, and the child tries to find the tree.

But how to arrange the pairs? If we put children together who had been having difficulty with one another and they violated trust, it was altogether likely that cooperative games would not be energized into healing intensity. If, on the other hand, we allowed the "best friends" who formed the core of the cliques to pair off, then there was the probability that those cliques would be reinforced.

The understanding of how the students were connected had been developing in us during the time the previous games were played. We relied on no other person's judgment, not even that of the teacher. It is in the course of the games, while involvement is total, that the child will forget the more superficial aspects of image, and will react according to needs. For instance, two boys who were often the object of one another's aggression had greatly enjoyed being paired in "Rolling Along." They moved across the field so quickly that the other children were delighted and stopped to watch them. Everyone was surprised, and comfortable, when they realized the new roles these boys were living.

In every group there are those who have the capability of providing a "neutralizing" influence. Often, this capability is hidden, for there is great pressure to join one side or another. In this class of first and second graders, the neutralizers were well underground. Communication and "safe space" had deteriorated to that extent. But we had spotted them during the group games. They played the games for the enjoyment of it, and did not worry who was next to them. They looked to us for information as to how best to play, and were not afraid of telling those who interfered to be quiet.

The biggest clue to the identity of the "neutralizers" was their need to let us know they were not identified with any one group of children. They let us know in subtle and not-so-subtle ways. One child would deliberately stand apart from the group while awaiting the next round of play. Another would deliberately join in with a child or group she didn't usually join, and would give us a verbal sign that she was doing so.

The "neutralizers" played a critical role in the games which followed. We split the more closely attached of the cliques among them. The rest we arranged so that they were with children they weren't ordinarily with, or ones with whom they had moderate difficulties. It worked out very well. By now our allotted time was spent and it was with a groan of displeasure that the children returned to the classroom.

Over the next few weeks, the parent who was in charge of the playground was trained. Gradually, more and more complex games were introduced, each time expanding the children's perception of safe space. Eventually we played games like "Cast Your Vote" and "Interview," in which they could express their understanding of, and desire for, their classroom. To do so took great courage on their parts, and it was not readily forthcoming. There were other difficulties in the relationship of the classroom teacher and the parents, but finally the class reached a place where, at least in the playground, they could channel their energy into cooperation.

Principles of Application

Cooperative games are a tool, and like all tools, they must be used with skill and sensitivity. One of the beautiful and exciting aspects of cooperative games and activities is that they can be varied according to the ages and talents of the participants; they can be adapted to every learning situation. Vary the games to fit the profile of the participants.

Age is a factor for each game. Please do not take age guidelines literally; experiment, and enjoy as you go along. But it is important to consider age, and at a deeper level, the growth stage of the children.

A thorough and meaningful understanding of the growth stages of children is one of the best tools for all education. Success with these games depends in large measure on your understanding of child development. With this understanding, games can be chosen and applied with an efficacy that is astounding.

The attitude of the game leader is critical. Children are naturally attuned to accept guidance from leaders, and so are able to read us in disarmingly straightforward ways. If the leader does not genuinely wish for cooperation, or in any way exhibits prejudice or manipulation, the playing of cooperative games becomes hypocritical. *As you model, so you teach.*

If a game does not work well the first time, come back to it later. Sometimes it takes several attempts before children grasp the sense of the games. Cooperative games and activities are not woven into the fabric of American play. Children have not been watching the games on TV since they were born. Therefore, go slowly. Do not attempt too many variations immediately. That creates the image of desperation. It is better to try lots of different games. Be honest, be patient and elist the children's help.

If a child does not want to play, do not force her. Do not allow her to disrupt the group, either. Our experience has been that after observing, most children join, or find a different constructive activity. There is something about the cooperative nature of the event that increases a child's safe space. The atmosphere becomes gentler and the children sense it.

Go ahead and play. Read through the games once or twice, familiarize yourself with ones you are to play that day, and then go for it. Why not? You've got nothing to lose. Your ability to facilitate will come from experience, and will come rather quickly.

Bring your sense of humor. This is the most important point of all. Make jokes, even bad ones. Lighten up, play games and let everyone enjoy themselves. Humor is the most healthy environment for everyone, and one in which you will have access to the most information concerning the children.

Games in Different Situations

Cooperative games and activities have been used successfully in all learning environments, at parties, within the immediate family and the extended family, and at large group gatherings. We have played them with whole communities, camps, public and private schools, the disabled and homeschooling collectives. They provide an excellent focus that allows appreciation of everyone's abilities in a friendly, comfortable way. Self-esteem grows; the inner sense of peace and interconnectedness comes alive.

There are games that serve as icebreakers, as a medium for feelings, as concentration intensifiers, as artistic and thinking enhancers, and as group and individual centering techniques. With a minimum of effort and a maximum of fun, cooperative games provide a way to recognize and integrate the rhythms of the participants.

In the experience described at the beginning of this introduction the situation was conflict within a large school group. We would like to close with descriptions of two more experiences, each of a very different nature. These three examples hardly exhaust all the situations amenable to the use of cooperative games. Hopefully, taken together, they will stimulate you to find your own approach to using them. If you require more information, feel free to write to us. We are sure we can create an application suitable for your situation.

We have the honor of guiding a group of children on a nature walk every Friday. There are about a dozen in the class ranging in age from 6 to 12. Our rhythm is to take an hour-long walk in the forest that surrounds our community, have a snack and then play cooperative games. We have lunch and then it is more games, or storytelling, or acting. The aim of the class is for the children to learn how to be friends. This aim they know. When conflict arises we stop our activity and work towards resolution. No cliques are allowed. We all agree that being friends is not all that easy. Every one of them is glad for the opportunity to learn. They are also angry that this skill is not usually taught for they clearly perceive the trouble grownups have relating.

Surprisingly, nature is not the primary attraction for the children. That honor belongs to cooperative games and activities, and the social dynamic arising there from. When we come across the red-tailed hawk doing a mating flight, or examine coyote scat to determine its diet, or surprise a flock of wild turkeys, or collect wildflowers to press, there is always great delight, wonder and appreciation of nature. But these are not sought. The children would rather play cooperative games. This, to us, is something of a shock, but a tribute to the power of these games in satisfying a genuine need of the children.

Their favorite game will not be found listed in this book. They created it themselves and, to be honest, we do not know all the rules. It is called "Wild Horses," and it has something to do with play acting horses, mountain lions, people, sheep, and whatever or whomever any participant wants to be. This game has evolved from a game they invented about the Greek myths. All we ask is that everyone be included, that there be no real violence and that no cliques form. At first there was some resistance to these guidelines, but now they need not even be mentioned. Every now and then we check in with different children to make sure they are included in a satisfactory way. We've yet to be disappointed.

"Wild Horses" did not appear until the class had been together over a year. We had gone through many games, most of them with success. Most games had their moment of being preferred, but, on the whole, each has had a similar amount of consideration. Often the children came up with their own variations.

One last experience concerns a mother and her six-year-old boy. We were asked to help when the mother was just concluding a painful and violent divorce from the boy's father. The boy — bright, energetic and sensitive — was having a difficult time in school. He is strong and likes the spotlight. His classmates had seized upon this to use him to personify their own negative tendencies. As a result, he was often dared and taunted. Like his father, he responded violently. The label of "bad" was hung on him and any time the others needed to participate in "badness," this boy was the chosen object.

And, to be sure, part of him liked it. It was attention and power, and even those who did not like him needed him. One boy, frail in body and underdeveloped emotionally, particularly enjoyed leaning on him, getting hit, and both of them being punished.

While work with this family proceeded on many levels, one small but important part involved cooperative games. We wanted to reawaken the boy's sense of belongingness. If he could feel that he belonged on this planet and in his family, then his life would be of value and destructive behaviors would diminish.

Two cooperative games were chosen and both worked very well. First, to give the mother the information on the disposition of the boy each day, an animal game was introduced around the breakfast table. The mother had many pictures of animals. Each morning she would hold one up and each person would say how they resembled that animal that day. She had everything from rearing cobras to cuddling koalas. There was a younger sister in the house, and the three of them would play together. Often they acted out their animal feelings. Of course, their moods became family knowledge and that instantly released some tension. And the mother had a much clearer picture of how to apply other remedies we were using in our attempt to improve the overall situation.

The other game was a morning family stretch game. Like the one above, it was very simple. Everyone meets by the fire for a five-minute stretch together, with each family member being the leader on a rotating basis. They soon added the variation of a hand coordination game. They now started their day taking a relaxed breath together. The connection that the boy needed to experience was present. He responded favorably and his good health was soon restored.

Friends, thank you for giving us the opportunity to write about cooperative games and activities. We truly hope you will experiment with them and find them as useful as we have. In this critical juncture of human evolution, they can help teach cooperation, respect and friendship. These are qualities that go a long way, and of which we can never get enough.

If we can be of any help to you, please do not hesitate to write.

Peace,

Ba Luvmour
Josette Luvmour

Preface to the Second Edition

WHEN NEW SOCIETY PUBLISHERS called to say they wanted to put out a new edition of this book, we were overjoyed. Since its first publication more than twenty years ago, Everyone Wins has had a profound impact on an incredibly diverse group of readers and their practices. Specifically, as reported by teachers, camp counselors, family coaches and youth group leaders, these games, activities and initiatives have had great value in evaluating interpersonal dynamics, teaching social justice, and assessing developmental capacities. In addition, the book has been used by child psychologists, dyslexia therapists, developmental psychologists and family therapists. It has been sold in many countries, is included in the national data bank on conflict resolution, and won the Parent's Choice Award. We never would have guessed that a little book that began on scraps of paper in my back pocket would have such an incredible impact on so many great people.

When this book was first published we were just beginning our nonprofit work. Starting with the Center for Educational Guidance our nonprofit, now called EnCompass, has grown tremendously. Over the years we have lead hundreds of parenting workshops, established the field of experiential learning programs for whole families, and given lectures and talks around the world. EnCompass is now operating out of Portland, Oregon where we are poised to actualize our ultimate vision: The EnCompass Institute.

The EnCompass Institute is a powerful vision of education built to strengthen the American family. The Institute uses Natural Learning Rhythms, the nationally recognized developmental model created by Ba and Josette Luvmour, as its philosophical basis. With its Lab School, Family Learning Center and Research Core, the EnCompass Institute integrates child development, family dynamics, teacher training, parent education, whole-family experiential learning and parent-teacher communication. The synergy of these parts come together in one place to create a powerful community of families experiencing optimal well-being and capable of changing the world.

We wish to dedicate this second addition to all the children. May they actualize their ultimate potential and live in well-being.

Enjoy!
Ba and Josette Luvmour, 2006
Portland, Oregon

EnCompass
www.EnCompassFamilies.org
Connection@EnCompassFamilies.org
800-200-1107

Ba Luvmour
www.BaLuvmour.com
503-929-7529

How to Use This Book

UNDER THE NAME OF EACH GAME you will find four categories containing information to help you evaluate its usefulness in different situations. These categories are:

Activity Level
"1" is the most active and "5" is the least active. The games are arranged by activity level. You will find the activities listed in order from 1 to 5.

Age
Age refers to the minimum age a participant needs to be to enjoy the game. All games are indexed by age at the back of the book.

Location
"In" means the game is best played indoors. "Out" means it must be played outdoors. "In/Out" means the game can be played indoors or outdoors.

Group Size
This refers to the minimum amount of players necessary to play the game. All games are indexed by group size at the back of the book.

How to Use the Indices

Games within an index are in alphabetical order. Thus if you want to find a game that needs six players, go to the Games Group Size Index and look up "Six or More Players." The games are alphabetically listed. If your players are seven and eight years old, then go to the Games Age Level Index, look up the age and cross reference with those games selected from the Games Group Size index. You are now ready to play.

The body of the game information consists of the *Description, Variations* and *Special Hints.* If *Materials* are needed, they are indicated in this section as well. Don't be afraid to try your own variations — and please drop us a line with any new hints you may discover in your play!

Activity Level 1

Chase in the Ocean

Activity Level: 1 Age Level: 4+
Location: In/Out Group Size: 6

Game Description:

A caller shouts "ship": and all the children run to the base at which she points. After counting three, the caller chases with arms outspread ready to gobble any child not on the base and touching another. The caller — if older — usually just misses.

Variations:

Sardine: All the children must be on base and touching one another.

Crab: The children must be back to back with one another.

Special Hints:

Make three or four areas to run to so caller can surprise the children by pointing as she calls.

Smaug's Jewels

Activity Level: 1 Age Level: 4+
Location: In/Out Group Size: 5
Materials: A rag

Game Description:

The "treasure" — a rag — is placed on the ground. One child guards it. All the others try to grab it. If a thief is touched by the guardian of the treasure she takes three steps back.

Variations:

Play with two guardians and have the tagged thief take five steps back.

Special Hints:

Be the referee.

Dho – Dho – Dho

Activity Level: 1 Age Level: 7+
Location: In/Out Group Size: 8

Game Description:
Two teams face off. While holding her breath, one player from a team crosses the line and tries to tag one or more players and make it back to her side; all the time holding her breath and with enough air left to say Dho-Dho-Dho. All tagged players switch teams. If the player does not succeed she joins the other team.
Variations:
Vary playing area size.
Special Hints:
Not fully cooperative so monitor closely. Valuable for energetic ones to let off steam.

Giants-Wizards-Elves

Activity Level: 1 Age Level: 5+
Location: In/Out Group Size: 8

Game Description:
Two teams. Each team agrees on a posture for a giant, a wizard and an elf and shows it to the other team. Each huddles and decides which creature it will be. Teams come to center line and at the count of three make the chosen posture and say the creature's name. Wizards fool Giants. Giants beat Elves. Elves trick wizards. Whoever loses has to beat it back to their safety about 20 feet away from the center line before the other team catches them. Those caught switch teams.
Special Hints:
Similar to Rock-Paper-Scissors with action.

On Your Knees

Activity Level: 1 Age Level: 7+
Location: In/Out Group Size: 1

Game Description:
Kneel down with back straight. Lift heels towards rump and grab ankles. Take knee steps as you are now balanced on your kneecaps.
Variations:
Try it as a group — grabbing a partner's ankle in a relay race or a dance.
Special Hints:
Make sure no knees get hurt.

Emotional Relay Race

Activity Level: 1 Age Level: 9+
Location: In/Out Group Size: 12
Materials: Three bowls and three pieces of fruit

Game Description:
Three teams — each lined up behind the piece of fruit of its choice. Each player takes time to come up with their sound and movement for "sad," "angry" and "happy." The bowls are set distance away. Each player picks up the fruit — runs to the bowl — puts it down — does "angry" three times — runs back to the start — does "happy" twice — back to fruit for "sad" twice — brings the fruit back to the start — takes a bite — and on to the next player.
Variations:
Can substitute other emotions or do it in tandem.
Special Hints:
Players should be in a playful mood right from the start.

Hop as One

Activity Level: 1 Age Level: 5+
Location: In/Out Group Size: 5

Game Description:

Players in a line — except for the leader — lift and extend left leg so the person behind can grab ankle or heel. They then place right hand on right shoulder of person in front for support. Now it's hop time.

Variations:

Switch sides — do a dance — collective timing — over obstacles.

Special Hints:

Remind them of careful coordination. Practice before getting discouraged.

Blanket Volleyball

Activity Level: 1 Age Level: 8+
Location: Outside Group Size: 6
Materials: Blankets and balls

Game Description:

Players hold the edge of the blanket. They place a ball on the blanket. They then toss the ball up by cooperatively manipulating the blanket. They try to catch it in the middle of the blanket. Score is cumulative.

Variations:

Use volleyball or beach ball. Change blanket size; define boundaries; use net. Pass the ball between two groups with blankets.

Special Hints:

Switch positions on blanket; make sure little ones do not get hurt. Skill needed. Greatly helps energetic ones to center on cooperation.

Upside Down Cycling

Activity Level: 1 Age Level: 4+
Location: In/Out Group Size: 2

Game Description:
Lie on back and touch bottom of feet with bottom of partner's feet. Do simultaneous cycling action first in one direction then in another.
Variations:
Try three players; eyes closed; use music.
Special Hints:
Works well for all shapes and sizes of people — even those in conflict.

Dragon Dodge Ball

Activity Level: 1 Age Level: 5+
Location: Outside Group Size: 7+
Materials: Sponge balls or rubber balls

Game Description:
All join hands in a large circle. Two people form a Dragon. One, the head, stands upright. The other, the tail, holds the head's hips and sticks her fanny out. The others pass balls around and try to hit the Dragon's fanny. If a ball hits the ground it must be passed before being thrown at the Dragon. No player can hold a ball more than three seconds. Passer who sets up the hit becomes the new tail. The former tail becomes the head. Use at least two balls at a time.
Variations:
More dragons. Vary circle size.
Special Hints:
Warn against collisions. Excellent for working out aggression.

How Do You Do?

Activity Level: 1 Age Level: 8+
Location: Outside Group Size: 10

Game Description:

All but two players join hands and form a circle. The outside two are a lost ship looking for port. They choose a pair from the circle. Holding hands, the chosen pair and the outside pair run around the circle in opposite directions attempting to get back to the vacant spot. As they pass one another, they must stop, shake hands and say "How do you do?" before continuing.

Variations:

Hop or skip around the circle. Travel with eyes closed and runners touching the circle as they move.

Special Hints:

Explain rules and direction of travel carefully. Warn against crashes. Make sure all get a turn.

Up and Around

Activity Level: 1 Age Level: 8+
Location: Outside Group Size: 2
Materials: Two-foot stick; belts; string; rubber ball

Game Description:

With a string tied to a broomstick, hang a tennis ball just above the ground. Children support the stick at their waists against their belts. Without using their hands they try to swing the ball over the stick.

Variations:

Make it wind and unwind. Play with eyes closed.

Special Hints:

Let little ones use their hands.

Blow the Ball

Activity Level: 1 Age Level: 4+
Location: Inside Group Size: 5
Materials: Ping pong ball and mats or blankets

Game Description:
One child lies on stomach on a mat. Six others grab edges of the mat and pull while the child blows the ping pong ball across the room. How fast can they do it?
Variations:
As a relay race with or without obstacles.
Special Hints:
Make sure no one player is overburdened.

Go Tag

Activity Level: 1 Age Level: 8+
Location: Outside Group Size: 10

Game Description:
Everyone squats in a line. Alternate players facing opposite directions, to the right and left. Everyone but person in front — *the chaser* — or back — *the chased* — kneels. The chaser can tap a squatter who then takes up the chase. The first chaser takes the squatter's position. The chaser must always go in the same direction. The chased can go in either direction. For example: Players 1 – 10 line up. Players 1, 3, 5, 7, 9 face to the right. Players 2, 4, 6, 8, 10 face to the left. Player 1 chases 10. If 1 decides that 7 has a better chance to tag 10, she taps 7 and takes her place. Player 7 takes up the chase. It's a game of timing and cunning.
Special Hints:
Practice a few times so all understand. Give everyone a chance to do everything.

It

Activity Level: 1   Age Level: 6+
Location: Outside   Group Size: 16

Game Description:
Two teams. Each goes to a different tree, leaving about 150 feet between them. One player calls It and starts running toward the other tree. If she touches the tree she scores a point. But anyone who touches her or is touched by her automatically becomes It. She can deliberately touch another on her team, who then continues toward the same goal. But if touched by a member of the other team, It is transferred and that player tries to move to her tree. No one can block or help the runner as she advances toward her tree.
Special Hints:
It is as if a spirit is being transferred at touch. Points are hard to score but not impossible.

Cooperative Relay Races

Activity Level: 1   Age Level: 5+
Location: Outside   Group Size: 8+
Materials: Varies according to type of race

Game Description:
Divide children into teams. They race for a best collective time while negotiating a course.
Variations:
Obstacles; crawling; running backwards; skipping; with golf ball in a spoon.
Special Hints:
Let children make up their own order of running; be prepared for it to get crazy.

True or False

Activity Level: 1 Age Level: 7+
Location: Outside Group Size: 8

Game Description:
Two teams, "Trues" and "Falses," face off in the middle of a field with a safety area for each team about 20 feet behind. Leader makes a statement about nature. If correct, Trues chase Falses. If incorrect, Falses chase Trues. Anyone caught goes to the other team.
Variations:
Statements about academics; or any other subject.
Special Hints:
Let confusion reign before supplying the correct answer. Choose questions appropriate to knowledge of players. This is an excellent teaching game.

Big Toe

Activity Level: 1 Age Level: 7+
Location: In/Out Group Size: 1

Game Description:
Squat down, grab your toes, bend your knees and try to jump forward as far as possible.
Variations:
Do it as a collective long jump or choreograph as a dance.
Special Hints:
You'll improve with practice. It is funny as a group.

Pull Together

Activity Level: 1 Age Level: 5+
Location: Outside Group Size: 10
Materials: Large strong rope

Game Description:
Leader divides children into two equal teams so when they pull on the rope as hard as they can, neither team moves.
Variations:
Tie a rope around a heavy object and try to move it.

Toby Terrific Turtle

Activity Level: 1 Age Level: 6+
Location: Outside Group Size: 5
Materials: Obstacles; green clothes; old blanket

Game Description:
Group huddles under blanket. All are blindfolded except the leader. Group moves together through obstacles as quickly as possible. Everyone gets a chance to be leader.
Variations:
Play in mud puddles! Group can hold hands.
Special Hints:
Be careful!

Catch the Dragon's Tail

Activity Level: 1 Age Level: 7+
Location: Outside Group Size: 8
Materials: Handkerchief

Game Description:
Players line up with arms around the waist of the person in front. Last one has a handkerchief in her pocket. The player at the head of the line tries to grab the handkerchief. No part of the Dragon may break.
Variations:
Two Dragons attempt to catch each other's tails. Rotate the players

Hug Tag

Activity Level: 1   Age Level: 4+
Location: Outside   Group Size: 8
Materials: Strips of cloth and hats or easily held objects

Game Description:
About one-sixth of the group are given strips of cloth. They are "It" and can tag any other player. The others are safe only when hugging another player. If two or more players keep hugging, "It" can take three steps backwards and say "1-2-3 Break!" Those players have to find new players to hug.
Special Hints:
Pick boundaries carefully. Keep the game moving. Great fun for everyone. Equalizes varied talents.

Obstacle Course

Activity Level: 1   Age Level: 3+
Location: Outside   Group Size: 5
Materials: Anything and everything

Game Description:
Children design their own obstacle course and run it.
Variations:
Infinite.
Special Hints:
Make sure all who want to participate have a chance to do so.

Creative Monkey Bars

Activity Level: 1   Age Level: 6+
Location: Outside   Group Size: 3
Materials: PVC pipe and fittings.

Game Description:
Using PVC pipe and fittings, children design and construct and play on their own monkey bars.
Variations:
Make their own furniture.
Special Hints:
Materials can be expensive, but self-esteem is worth it! Switch children around so that balance is achieved. When they get the idea, encourage them to switch themselves.

Couples Sports

Activity Level: 1 Age Level: 8+
Location: Outside Group Size: 10
Materials: Balls and leg ties

Game Description:
Play baseball with legs tied together or holding hands.
Variations:
Any ball game or tag.
Special Hints:
Match pairs with attention to athletic ability. Use small playing space.

MJ Jessen

Activity Level 2

Come Together

Activity Level: 2 | Age Level: 5+
Location: Inside or outside | Group Size: 2

Game Description:
Two players stand at opposite ends of a room, then run toward each other and leap. The object is to land as close as possible without touching one another.
Variations:
Land side by side. Shake hands while passing in the air. Turn around in the air and land close together.
Special Hints:
Needs several practice attempts before it becomes a game. Be careful.

Snowblind

Activity Level: 2 | Age Level: 5+
Location: Inside or outside | Group Size: 5
Materials: A long foam sword or suitable padded substitute

Game Description:
It is blindfolded and has the sword, and chants for 10 seconds. The rest of the players run inside the boundaries and assume stationary crouch when the chanting stops. It moves around trying to tag players with the sword.
Variations:
Players stay still after chant stops. Anyone tagged joins It and next round begins with the Its chanting and players moving.
Special Hints:
Make sure sword is soft. Modify boundaries according to the abilities of the players.

Lemonade

Activity Level: 2 | Age Level: 4+
Location: Inside or outside | Group Size: 8

Game Description:
Two teams, each with a safety area about 20 feet behind them, face off in the middle. One team has decided on the role (e.g., astronauts, clowns, scuba divers, etc.) they are going to pantomime. When someone guesses right, the pantomimists race for their safety area. The other team chases. Anyone tagged switches teams.
Variations:
Include scenes from nature, literature or fantasy roles (e.g., clouds).
Special Hints:
Help the little ones. Everyone loves this game; it brings groups together.

Hawk and Mouse

Activity Level: 2 | Age Level: 6+
Location: Inside or outside | Group Size: 6

Game Description:
Two blindfolded children are in the middle of the circle. One is a local predator, the other is its prey. The rest of the children keep them safely in the circle. The predator tries to find the prey who has a little bell around her neck. No talking.
Variations:
Anytime predator makes its sound, prey must answer.
Special Hints:
Make the circle smaller if the predator has trouble finding the prey. Remind the children not to let anyone fall.

Amigos All

Activity Level: 2 Age Level: 5+
Location: Inside or outside Group Size: 7
Materials: Bean bags

Game Description:
Children walk at their own pace balancing a bean bag on their head. Leader controls the pace. If bean bag falls, the child is frozen. Another child must pick up the bean bag and place it on the frozen child's head, without losing her own.
Variations:
Many movements. Introduce obstacles. Cooperative relay race. Use music. Give children an opportunity to lead and come up with their own variations.
Special Hints:
If too difficult, let little ones use one hand.

Don't Use Your Teeth

Activity Level: 2 Age Level: 6+
Location: Ouside Group Size: 3
Materials: Tube sock or old towel

Game Description:
One player stands a short distance from the other two and throws a knotted sock or towel toward them. They have to catch it with their bodies, but without using their hands.
Variations:
Back to back. One of the two catchers closes her eyes.
Special Hints:
A good way to let active children who are having trouble being together work it out.

Up and Over

Activity Level: 2 Age Level: 5+
Location: Inside or outside Group Size: 10

Game Description:
Divide the children into small groups of various sizes. Each group makes itself into a human obstacle. Players then have to run the course. When they get to an obstacle, the obstacle tells them how to get past it. As players pass an obstacle, they join the end of the line to traverse remaining obstacles. As group finishes the course, it makes a new obstacle while all other players are still on previous obstacles. It can go on this way for hours.
Variations:
Add non-human obstacles. Allow no talking. Increase number of people comprising each obstacle. Add skills such as dribbling a ball while running the course.
Special Hints:
Watch carefully and learn about your players; much is revealed in this activity.

Standing Together

Activity Level: 2 Age Level: 8+
Location: Inside or outside Group Size: 4

Game Description:
Seated in a circle, players grasp arms or hands and try to collectively stand up.
Variations:
Larger groups. Grabbing people not next to one another.
Special Hints:
Let the group experiment. Go slowly; the more people, the harder it is.

Octopus

Activity Level: 2 Age Level: 4+
Location: Inside or outside Group Size: 5

Game Description:
In a defined area, one child is the Octopus. He attempts to tag another. When he does, that child is frozen but can wave her arms like the tentacles of an octopus, helping tag others until all are Octopi.
Variations:
All the tag variations. Vary play area size and location.
Special Hints:
Use big boundaries.

Walking Together

Activity Level: 2 Age Level: 8+
Location: Ouside Group Size: 3
Materials: 2 ten-foot long 2x4" studs;
12 four-inch long leather straps or nylon webbing;
screws

Game Description:
Six leather straps — for footholds — are screwed into each stud. Six people slip their feet into the straps — left feet in one "sandal," right feet in the other — and try to walk as a unit.
Variations:
Move over or through obstacles. Dance. Move sideways. Try indoors with pieces of carpet. Try various lengths of studs.
Special Hints:
Make sure they practice before trying difficult maneuvers. Be safe.

Beam Walk

Activity Level: 2	Age Level: 5+
Location: Inside or outside	Group Size: 1

Game Description:
Children practice on balance beams, such as on supported 4x4s. Many cooperative possibilities to try.

Variations:
Music, obstacles, pairs, etc.

Special Hints:
Be safe! Builds self-esteem if approached gently.

Base Ball Pass

Activity Level: 2 Age Level: 7+
Location: Outside Group Size: 8
Materials: Large balls

Game Description:
Four players and one large ball start at each of four bases. Two players move their ball to the next base without using hands and pass the ball to the waiting pair. They then await the next pair coming behind them to pass them another ball, which they move to the next base and pass on.

Variations:
Three on a team. Vary number of bases.

Special Hints:
Keep the game moving. Help the slower ones.

Moving Ladder

Activity Level: 2 Age Level: 6+
Location: Ouside Group Size: 6
Materials: Sturdy ladder

Game Description:
Players spread out along both sides of the ladder and lift it so that it is held horizontally at their waists. One end is lowered and the Traveler crawls on to it. The ladder is raised and the Traveler crawls the length of the ladder.

Variations:
Use a plank. Change the angle of the ladder. Walk the ladder around.

Special Hints:
Watch for tiring ladder holders and for show-offs.

Snake in the Grass

Activity Level: 2 Age Level: 5+
Location: Inside or outside Group Size: 5

Game Description:
One player is the Snake in the grass, and lies and slithers around on her belly. All the other players touch one part of the Snake's body. When ready, trying to surprise the other players, the Snake says "Snake in the grass!" and tries to tag players. Anyone tagged becomes a Snake, until all are tagged.

Variations:
Change boundaries. Allow Snakes to be Alligators or Bears (move on hands and knees).

Special Hints:
Shoes off if possible. Keep the players challenging the Snake.

Log Pass

Activity Level: 2 Age Level: 7+
Location: Ouside Group Size: 8
Materials: Big log

Game Description:
Each player gets a number, starting with one. Players line up on a log in order. Now Player 1 must switch places with the last player (from the other end), without falling off the log. Then Player 2 switches places with the next-to-last player, and so on, until all have switched.

Variations:
Try with various conditions, for instance no talking, switchers blindfolded or one hand on top of head, etc.

Special Hints:
Make instructions clear at the beginning. Be safe!

Shape Tag

Activity Level: 2 Age Level: 6+
Location: Ouside Group Size: 5

Game Description:
Three players form a triangle. A forth is It and a fifth tries to avoid being tagged. The triangle protects the fifth by changing shapes.
Variations:
Make play area boundaries with no tagging across the triangle. Players making triangle keep hands on each other's shoulders. Try multiple triangles with equal number of chasers and chased. Let any chaser catch anyone being chased.
Special Hints:
Change boundaries so no one is It for too long. Shape Tag can slip into competitiveness, so be careful.

Cooperative Juggle

Activity Level: 2 Age Level: 8+
Location: Inside or outside Group Size: 5
Materials: Balls

Game Description:
Player 1 throws ball to any other player. The receiver says her name as she catches it. She then throws to another, who after saying his name, throws it to another, until all have had one chance. As the ball goes around a second time, the thrower says the name of the person to whom she is throwing. Players throw to same person each time. Keep adding balls to see how many can be juggled. Each time a ball is thrown, the thrower must call the name of the receiver. Player 1 initiates each ball.

Variations:
Large groups or small. Use yarn, socks, or anything soft. Cooperative Juggle is group juggling with many objects being thrown to everyone; all the thrower has to do is establish eye contact with the receiver.
Special Hints:
Good icebreaker; lots of fun. Let those having conflict play by themselves with many balls.

Wheelbarrow

Activity Level: 2 | Age Level: 6+
Location: Inside or outside | Group Size: 2+

Game Description:
In pairs, one child holds both legs of the other while that child moves on his hands.
Variations:
Choreograph movements of one or several pairs. Introduce obstacles, blindfolds, etc.
Special Hints:
Make sure each goes at their own speed. Switch partners.

Garden

Activity Level: 2 Age Level: 1+
Location: Outside Group Size: 1
Materials: Compost; fertilizers; shovels; seeds; soil; water; fencing (if necessary)

Game Description:
Make an organic garden of whatever size is appropriate. Make it as a family, school, group, class or community effort.
Variations:
Herb gardens. Seed gardens. Sprout gardens. Wildflower gardens.
Special Hints:
Grow something year round.

One Big Slug

Activity Level: 2 Age Level: 4+
Location: Inside or outside Group Size: 4
Materials: Mats, things for an obstacle course

Game Description:
Children build an obstacle course. Then they connect into groups of four and, while holding the ankles of the one in front, go through the course on hands and knees.
Variations:
Cover all their bodies but heads with a blanket.

Cooperative Musical Chairs

Activity Level: 2 Age Level: 3+
Location: Inside or outside Group Size: 5
Materials: Music and floor pillows

Game Description:
Just like musical chairs, except that when the music stops

and one pillow is removed, the remaining players all have to sit or touch the remaining pillows.

Variations:

Have all players sit on top of one another. Be careful that no one gets hurt.

Popcorn Balls

Activity Level: 2 — Age Level: 3+
Location: Inside or outside — Group Size: 7

Game Description:

Children crouch on the floor. Everyone chants: "Popcorn balls, popcorn balls, popcorn balls,"sounding like a locomotive. Adult tells the children that as the pan (the floor) starts to heat up, the popcorn (the children) starts popping (children hopping) all over the place. When two children bump each other while popping, they stick together. The game is over when all are one ball.

Special Hints:

Good for the little ones.

See Saw

Activity Level: 2 — Age Level: 8+
Location: Inside or outside — Group Size: 2

Game Description:

Facing one another, partners sit with knees bent up and bottoms of their feet on the floor. They slip their feet just under the other's behind, join hands, and move by back and forward rocking motion.

Variations:

Reverse directions. Make it a co-op relay race. Use obstacles.

Special Hints:

End by coming to a standing position.

Rope Raising

Activity Level: 2 | Age Level: 8+
Location: Inside or outside | Group Size: 10
Materials: Long rope tied at its ends to form a circle

Game Description:
Seated in a circle, group all pulls on the rope with their hands, so that they can all stand at once.
Variations:
Stretch rope out in a line and make two equal teams at ends. Pull together so that everyone stands up.
Special Hints:
Coach the children to pull together. Watch out for the energetic children criticizing the less active ones.

Rolling Along

Activity Level: 2 | Age Level: 3+
Location: Inside or outside | Group Size: 2

Game Description:
In pairs, partners lie stretched out on the floor, toe to toe, heads in opposite direction. They attempt to roll across the floor, keeping toes connected.
Variations:
Only toes of one foot connected. Try while sitting in an "L" position.
Special Hints:
Keep sending one pair down after the last. Use verbal encouragement. Select pairs carefully.

Dolphin and Fish

Activity Level: 2 | Age Level: 5+
Location: Inside or outside | Group Size: 8

Game Description:
All but two players circle and hold hands. One free player is a Dolphin and the other is a Fish. Dolphin chases Fish. When Fish runs through the circle, children raise their arms; but when Dolphin tries to get through, they lower them.
Special Hints:
No favoritism among the children. Help the slow by altering the rules.

All of Us, All at Once

Activity Level: 2 Age Level: 1+
Location: Inside or outside Group Size: 2
Materials: Anything and everything

Game Description:
Leader suggests a thing to be, and the group "is" that thing collectively.
Variations:
As varied as your imagination.
Special Hints:
Perfect for integrating new people and different ages.

Blind Trail

Activity Level: 2 Age Level: 8+
Location: Outside Group Size: 6
Materials: Rope and blindfolds

Game Description:
Blindfolded players are guided through a part of the forest by feeling their way along a rope that has been placed there by the leader. The leader removes the rope when players get to the end. Players uncover their eyes and find their way back to the starting point.

Variations:
Across level areas, a stream, over logs. If players are old enough, use a very long rope.
Special Hints:
Emphasize calm awareness. Vary complexity.

Dances of the Mind

Activity Level: 2	Age Level: 3+
Location: Inside or outside	Group Size: 3+

Game Description:
Have the children form a dance as an expression of a chosen concept, for instance high-low and medium.
Variations:
Colors. Time. Relatives, aggressions, etc. Use music as appropriate. Let the older ones pick their own.
Special Hints:
Help them along. Filter sarcasm. Once in progress, a great builder of self-esteem and non-verbal communication skills.

MJ Jessen

Activity Level 3

What Does This Mean?

Activity Level: 3 Age Level: 5+
Location: Inside or outside Group Size: 4
Materials: Anything and everything

Game Description:
Each player is told to find an object that has a special value for her. Discussion follows during which each child tells how the object exemplifies her value. For example, a rock represents friendship because of its solidity, or the moon is caring due to lighting the earth at night.
Variations:
Restrict objects to nature. Agree on one value for the entire class and have everyone find different representations of it.
Special Hints:
Give examples. Encourage free expression. Participate yourself.

Where Were You?

Activity Level: 3 Age Level: 5+
Location: Inside or outside Group Size: 12

Game Description:
Leader stands in the middle. Children are in four teams on her left, right, in front and behind. Children are still while leader turns in a circle and stops. Then teams reposition themselves as they were before — on the left, right, front and back.
Variations:
Collectively time them.
Special Hints:
Best to have 16 or 20 children.

Rhythm Sticks

Activity Level: 3 Age Level: 6+
Location: Inside or outside Group Size: 2
Materials: Cut one-inch dowels about 18" long

Game Description:
Children sit cross-legged facing one another. They establish a rhythm with their sticks by hitting their own sticks together, hitting the floor, hitting each other's sticks. Then, do it to music.
Variations:
Vary group size. Use one hand only. Let the children sing their own music. Try it blindfolded.
Special Hints:
Play along and have fun. Vary the ages playing together. Let some children make music with other instruments. Enhances musical and non-verbal communication skills.

Still Photograph

Activity Level: 3 Age Level: 8+
Location: Inside or outside Group Size: 4

Game Description:
One player takes a few members of the group and tells them of an experience when she was happy. She then places them in a frozen picture recalling that time. The rest of the group has to guess the situation.
Variations:
Other emotions. Vary group size. Share tableaux with the larger group.
Special Hints:
Encourage detail. Stimulates compassion. Group children having difficulty together.

Wheel

Activity Level: 3 Age Level: 4+
Location: Inside or outside Group Size: 5

Game Description:
All players stand sideways in a circle and put hands toward the middle. They are now spokes of a wheel. Turn and move around the room.
Variations:
Hopping and/or skipping. Over obstacles. Eyes closed.
Special Hints:
Increase complexity to keep interest high. Best for the very young.

Stiff as a Board

Activity Level: 3 Age Level: 5+
Location: Inside or outside Group Size: 5

Game Description:
One player lies on the ground as stiffly as possible. The others pick her up and carry her as far as they can.
Variations:
Make it a relay race. Introduce obstacles. Balance a glass of water on the back of the one being carried.
Special Hints:
Make sure no one is straining. No jokes or put-downs about another child's anatomy.

Down the Tube

Activity Level: 3 Age Level: 5+
Location: Inside or outside Group Size: 2
Materials: Ping pong ball, cardboard tube such as from toilet tissue roll

Game Description:
Toss the ball back and forth, trying to catch it in the tube.
Variations:
Use a ring instead of ping pong ball and try to catch it on a stick. Vary distance between players or hand used in game.

Down the Hole

Activity Level: 3 Age Level: 5+
Location: Inside or outside Group Size: 6
Materials: Old sheet or bedspread and a ball

Game Description:
Cut a small hole, just big enough for the ball, in the center of the sheet. Children hold the edges of the sheet and try to get the ball to go through the hole.
Variations:
Use several balls, try a parachute instead of a sheet.
Special Hints:
Great fun; brings the group to a "center."

Hello, But I'm Gone

Activity Level: 3 Age Level: 4+
Location: Inside or outside Group Size: 7

Game Description:
Children sit in a circle with one standing on the outside. She pats someone on the head and each runs in opposite directions around the circle. When they meet they must stop, shake hands and say "Hello, but I'm gone." The first player runs and sits down and the second proceeds around the circle and repeats the game.
Special Hints:
Great fun for the little ones.

Use that Rope

Activity Level: 3 Age Level: 3+
Location: Inside or outside Group Size: 4
Materials: Rope

Game Description:
Using jump ropes, children make letters, numbers, geometric shapes, flowers, etc.
Variations:
Change size of rope. Vary number of children and ways in which rope shapes interrelate.
Special Hints:
Fade into background, but stay close to help maintain flow.

Alternate Leaning

Activity Level: 3 Age Level: 6+
Location: Inside or outside Group Size: 20

Game Description:
Stand in a circle with arms linked. Alternate people are "ins" and "outs." At the signal, players lean either in or out. By supporting one another, a steep lean can be achieved.
Variations:
Hold hands. Do it in rhythm.
Special Hints:
Keep feet stationary. The more people the better.

Hold Me Up

Activity Level: 3 Age Level: 7+
Location: Inside or outside Group Size: 2

Game Description:
Partners face off and then slowly fall away and catch one

another by the arm — pull up close and then fall away again and catch by another part of the arm.

Variations:

One arm or two arms. Try groups of three or four.

Special Hints:

Go slow and make sure all are comfortable.

How Many are Standing?

Activity Level: 3 Age Level: 4+
Location: Inside or outside Group Size: 8

Game Description:

Sit in a circle. Anyone stands up whenever they want to, but cannot remain standing longer than five seconds. Aim of the game is to have exactly four standing at one time.

Variations:

Vary group size and amount standing, or time standing up.

Special Hints:

Great for an icebreaker and for the little ones.

Feeling Sculpture

Activity Level: 3 Age Level: 8+
Location: Inside or outside Group Size: 4

Game Description:

Partner A whispers a feeling word into partner B's ear. B sculpts A into a representation of that feeling. After one minute they find another pair. Each pair tries to guess the other's feeling. Add charades if necessary.

Variations:

Do it in groups.

Special Hints:

Don't forget to shape the face.

Strike the Pose

Activity Level: 3 Age Level: 6+
Location: Inside or outside Group Size: 8

Game Description:
Two leave the room. The rest of the group decides on a pose that is specific but not too detailed. The two come back in and begin striking poses. The group signals hot or cold until the two strike the group pose.
Variations:
Only one leaves the room.
Special Hints:
Vary pose complexity according to age level. Many moves should be tried at first until the group reacts.

Spaghetti

Activity Level: 3 Age Level: 6+
Location: Inside or outside Group Size: 6

Game Description:
All stand in a circle. Join hands, but not with the person on either side. Now untangle without letting go of hands.
Special Hints:
Sometimes it cannot be done. Give all a chance to move people around. See introduction.

Find Your Animal Mate

Activity Level: 3 Age Level: 3+
Location: Inside or outside Group Size: 8

Game Description:
Animal names are written on a piece of paper. Each animal is named twice. The children are each given a slip so

they know only their animal. They then act out the animal, while trying to find their partner. When two find each other, they ask the leader if they are right.

Variations:

Without sounds.

Gyrating Reptile

Activity Level: 3 Age Level: 4+
Location: Inside or outside Group Size: 5

Game Description:

Children lie on the floor and grab the ankles of the child in front of them, making one big snake. Then, gyrating energetically, they try to move across the floor.

Variations:

Over obstacles. Against time.

Special Hints:

Ask the children for ideas.

Nature Acting

Activity Level: 3 Age Level: 3+
Location: Inside or outside Group Size: 4

Game Description:

A child acts out a real life situation, e.g., a butterfly drinking from a flower; or a teacher reprimanding a student. The others try to guess what it is.

Variations:

Use props. Let children act in groups.

Special Hints:

Encourage children to come up with their own ideas, but be there to help. Don't let anyone make fun by putting down another.

Animal Acting

Activity Level: 3 Age Level: 3+
Location: Inside or outside Group Size: 5

Game Description:
Children choose an animal and act it out. Others try to guess what it is.
Variations:
Have the animal doing something. Use sounds.
Special Hints:
Let the children choose their own animals, if possible.

Tied Together

Activity Level: 3 Age Level: 5+
Location: Inside or outside Group Size: 6

Game Description:
Two children hide their eyes. The others join hands and make themselves into the craziest knot they can. The two open their eyes and try to undo the knot without breaking handholds.
Variations:
Eyes closed.
Special Hints:
Make sure all get a chance to be the undoers.

Blind Walks

Activity Level: 3 Age Level: 6+
Location: Inside or outside Group Size: 2
Materials: Blindfolds
Game Description:
In pairs, with one blindfolded, the children lead one another.

Variations:
Obstacles. Do it in nature.
Special Hints:
Builds self-esteem to trust and be trusted. Instruct to be careful.

Face to Face

Activity Level: 3 | Age Level: 3+
Location: Inside or outside | Group Size: 2

Game Description:
Partners stand a couple of feet apart. One closes her eyes and gently moves forward, trying to connect noses. The other stands still.
Variations:
Both have eyes closed.
Special Hints:
Good for special relationships. Introduce breathing as a clue.

In and Out

Activity Level: 3 | Age Level: 5+
Location: Inside or outside | Group Size: 2

Game Description:
Partners face one another with feet spread to shoulder width. With hands up, palms open, bodies rigid, the partners lean forward and catch one another. Then push off and spring back up.
Variations:
Vary distance to limit of capabilities.
Special Hints:
Play on soft surface. Match players consciously.

Rhythm Learning

Activity Level: 3 Age Level: 6+
Location: Inside or outside Group Size: 2
Materials: Large ball

Game Description:
In pairs, children pass a ball back and forth while calling out letters of the alphabet.
Variations:
Spell words. Names of animals or familiar people. Do simple mathematics.
Special Hints:
Keep a rhythm going, perhaps by handclapping, but do not make it too fast or exclude anyone.

Use that Body

Activity Level: 3 Age Level: 4+
Location: Inside or outside Group Size: 4

Game Description:
Together, the children make numbers, shapes, letters with their bodies. Everyone in the group must be included.
Special Hints:
Use small groups.

Move Softly

Activity Level: 3 Age Level: 8+
Location: Inside or outside Group Size: 6
Materials: Blindfold and a rag for treasure

Game Description:
One child sits on the ground, garding a treasure with the referee standing behind her. She "falls asleep" — wearing

a blindfold — and the others try to creep up as quietly as possible to steal the treasure. If the child hears someone, she points in that direction and everyone freezes. If the referee agrees that the child guarding the treasure pointed directly at the person, that person must take three steps backward.

Special Hints:

Be the referee, or allow a child to be the referee.

No-Hands Ball Pass

Activity Level: 3 | Age Level: 5+
Location: Inside or outside | Group Size: 5
Materials: Ball

Game Description:

Players sit on floor in tight circle and extend feet towards the center. A ball is placed on one player's lap. The idea is to move the ball around the circle as fast as possible without using hands.

Variations:

Vary the size and number of balls. Reverse the direction of the ball.

Special Hints:

Lots of fun. If it doesn't work the first time, try again.

Pasta

Activity Level: 3 | Age Level: 3+
Location: Inside | Group Size: 6

Game Description:

Players are a package of pasta, bundled close together. As pot boils, players begin to relax and eventually end up in a limp pile on the floor.

Blanket Toss

Activity Level: 3 Age Level: 6+
Location: Inside or outside Group Size: 6
Materials: Ballons and a blanket

Game Description:
Cut a hole in the blanket. Place balloons on it. Players grab edges of the blanket and try to maneuver the balloon through the hole.
Variations:
Can keep score, with smaller values given to smaller balloons and larger values given to larger balloons.
Special Hints:
Join the fun!

Strange Positions

Activity Level: 3 Age Level: 4+
Location: Inside Group Size: 5

Game Description:
The leader tells players to get into a strange position and hold it. The leader then tells them to get into a second strange position, and so on. Positions should involve more than one player.
Special Hints:
For the very young.

Wooden Children

Activity Level: 3 Age Level: 4+
Location: Outside Group Size: 8

Game Description:
Several players lie on their backs, totally stiff, being logs.

Others cooperate to lift these logs and place them as corner poles for a house, or put them in a stove. Players huddle in house or warm themselves around stove.

Variations:

Other pole applications. Other players dig imaginary holes for posts. Talk about the many gifts trees give us.

Shoe Mates

Activity Level: 3 Age Level: 6+
Location: Inside Group Size: 12

Game Description:

Players take off shoes and pile them in the middle. Each player selects an unmatched pair of shoes, neither of which are her own. All walk around trying to find shoe mates and stand next to people so that shoes are matched in pairs.

Special Hints:

Remind big people not to crush little toes.

Rocks in a Creek

Activity Level: 3 Age Level: 4+
Location: Inside or outside Group Size: 8

Game Description:

Players put hands on hips and slowly spin "downstream" together. As elbows touch, arms go down, simulating wearing down of sharp edges. Dizzy players crouch at bottom of creek, face upstream, extend arms back and wiggle open hands like rippling water.

Special Hints:

Talk about water as energy, transporting and rounding rocks.

Ocean Friends

Activity Level: 3 Age Level: 3+
Location: Inside or outside Group Size: 8
Materials: Beanbags

Game Description:
Fill rooms with (imaginary) water. Players swim around with beanbags on heads. Dropped bag means player freezes. Friend must take deep breath, dive down and replace bag. End by pulling plug and all whirlpool closer and closer to center.
Variations:
Practice deep breaths before starting. Children may use one finger to hold beanbag on.

Hold that Floor

Activity Level: 3 Age Level: 4+
Location: Inside Group Size: 5

Game Description:
Players run around until leader calls "freeze," and a number. Players must stop and touch the number of body parts to the floor that the leader called.
Variations:
When "freeze" is called, players have to find a partner and get the body parts down together.

Slow Motion Tag

Activity Level: 3 Age Level: 5+
Location: Inside or outside Group Size: 12

Game Description:
Slow motion tag. When tagged, a person joins It. When 4 players are joined as It, they split into pairs and tag

others. When everyone is tagged, all chant "A-moe-ba," so all will know that the game is over.

Variations:

Vary the split size of the It group, with overall number of players.

Special Hints:

Remember — move in slow motion.

A Chance to be Nice

Activity Level: 3 Age Level: 3+
Location: Inside or outside Group Size: 8+

Game Description:

Players line up facing one another. Taking turns each player skips down the line while the others say something nice about that person.

Special Hints:

Make sure no sarcasm surfaces. Wait until your group begins to feel good about one another. Come back to it later if it fails the first time. An easy way to say something nice about someone else.

Whose Shoe?

Activity Level: 3 Age Level: 6+
Location: Inside Group Size: 5
Materials: Shoes

Game Description:

Each child takes off one shoe and puts it in a pile. Everyone picks up someone else's shoe and, while somehow holding it, joins hands and forms a circle. Shoe owners are identified and shoes must be returned while holding hands.

Inuit Ball Pass

Activity Level: 3 Age Level: 8+
Location: Inside outside Group Size: 8

Game Description:
Players kneel in a circle and pass the ball from person to person with a flat, open hand (palm up). The aim is to move the ball as rapidly as possible around the circle without actually grasping it.
Variations:
Use more than one ball at a time.
Special Hints:
Learn to play with two hands first.

Don't Let Go

Activity Level: 3 Age Level: 5+
Location: Inside or outside Group Size: 2

Game Description:
Partners face off, extend arms and hold hands. Now move into positions that would leave each partner totally off-balance were it not for the support of the other.
Variations:
Support with different parts than hands. Try with more than two people.
Special Hints:
Tell each player to explore all kinds of new positions. Quiet music is nice. Builds trust.

Children's Carapace

Activity Level: 3 Age Level: 3+
Location: Inside Group Size: 5
Materials: Blanket and tarp or gym mat

Game Description:
The group gets on its hands and knees and tries to move a large shell (blanket) in one direction.
Variations:
Over an obstacle. Play out turtle stories.
Special Hints:
Give them time to realize they all need to move in the same direction.

Jump Jump Jump

Activity Level: 3 Age Level: 3+
Location: Outside Group Size: 5

Game Description:
Each child jumps in succession. The aim is to see how far the group can collectively jump.
Variations:
Over obstacles. Estimate the jumps to a certain spot.
Special Hints:
Vary the order in which children jump. Encourage them to beat their old mark.

All Paint

Activity Level: 3 Age Level: 4+
Location: Inside Group Size: 6
Materials: Large paper and paint

Game Description:
A shape is drawn on a large piece of paper. The paper is hung at a height such that the tallest in the group must jump her highest to reach the top of the shape. Children dip their fingers in paint and, jumping up, try to fill the shape in.

Variations:
Use letters or numbers as shapes.
Special Hints:
Vary heights in each group, making sure the shortest gets the bottom to fill. Teaches non-verbal sharing.

Probably Wet

Activity Level: 3 Age Level: 6+
Location: Outside Group Size: 6
Materials: Cups and water

Game Description:
Players stand in a circle with an empty paper cup in their teeth. One cup is filled with water, and players attempt to pass the water from cup to cup without spilling it. No hands.
Variations:
Fill more cups. Widen the circle.
Special Hints:
Make sure it is OK with each child to get wet.

Handle With Care

Activity Level: 3 Age Level: 4+
Location: Outside Group Size: 5
Materials: Big leaves

Game Description:
Players stand in line. A broad leaf is passed overhead until it reaches the back of the line. Then, that person brings it to the front and starts again. The aim is for everyone to be first, and not to damage the leaf.
Variations:
Play it with any natural object.

Special Hints:
Talk about leaves. Discuss ecology, and/or the damage humans do to nature.

Marble Tracking

Activity Level: 3 Age Level: 7+
Location: Outside Group Size: 3
Materials: PVC pipe and marbles

Game Description:
Cut 1" PVC pipe in half lengthwise to make a track. Use these tracks on a slope to make a downhill run for the marbles.
Variations:
Steep downhill. Slow switchbacks. Introduce obstacles.
Special Hints:
Help set it up. Participate yourself. Let the children make their own courses.

Path Finder

Activity Level: 3 Age Level: 5+
Location: Outside Group Size: 6

Game Description:
Divide players into two groups. Each group marks their own nature trail using only natural objects. Dots of flour are OK, but do not deface anything. Meet back at starting place and then each group follows the other's trail.
Variations:
Vary the terrain, including through water.
Special Hints:
Don't let one group make it too hard for the other until the game has been played a few times. Builds children's confidence in natural settings.

Sounds and Colors

Activity Level: 3 Age Level: 6+
Location: Outside Group Size: 4

Game Description:
In a natural setting, children lie on their backs with eyes closed. Every time one hears a new bird call, they raise a finger. Then, looking around with eyes open, do the same for new colors.

Variations:
Use any sounds. See if they can count to ten without hearing a new call or seeing a new color.

Special Hints:
Emphasize quietness.

Tree Silhouettes

Activity Level: 3 Age Level: 6+
Location: Outside Group Size: 5

Game Description:
In a place where several different tree types grow, have a child shape herself like a tree. The others try to guess which tree she is imitating.

Variations:
Use groups. Do any natural formation.

Special Hints:
Can be worked in with real life drama.

Hug a Tree

Activity Level: 3 Age Level: 5+
Location: Outside Group Size: 2
Materials: Blindfold

Game Description:
In pairs, one child leads another, who is blindfolded, to

a tree by a circuitous route. The blindfolded one explores the tree with all other senses, and then is led back to the starting point. Blindfold removed, she sets out to find her tree.

Variations:

Hug anything.

Special Hints:

Try to find a heavily wooded area. Talk about trees.

Unnature Trail

Activity Level: 3 Age Level: 6+
Location: Outside Group Size: 6
Materials: Various unnatural objects, such as paper clips or bobby pins

Game Description:
Along a trail, hide a dozen human-made objects. Some should be easy to find, others well hidden. The children try to find them, but do not touch them. They report their findings to the teacher, who sends them back to look for any they missed.
Special Hints:
Hide a paper bag well. It is unlikely it will be found, and will facilitate a discussion about camouflage, which is one of the aims of this activity.

Duplicate

Activity Level: 3 Age Level: 8+
Location: Outside Group Size: 4
Materials: Naturally occurring objects and a cloth

Game Description:
Collect several naturally occurring objects from the game area. Place them on the ground, covered by the cloth. Lifting the cloth for 30 seconds, let the children study the objects, then cover them again. Then, tell them to go find objects like them in the area.
Variations:
Vary time to study. Vary number of objects.
Special Hints:
Pull objects out one at a time to see who has the match. Careful not to let this game get competitive.

Prooie

Activity Level: 3
Location: Inside or outside
Age Level: 7+
Group Size: 10

Game Description:

Players scatter around a defined area. All close their eyes. Leader moves through the group and silently chooses one player to be "Prooie." Prooie opens her eyes. Leader gives a signal to begin. All except Prooie start wandering around, keeping their eyes closed. As they bump into each other, they say "Prooie?" If the person answers "Prooie," they separate and continue to wander. The object is to find the Prooie, who never answers back. When they bump into Prooie, ask their question, and receive no reply, they open their eyes and join hands with Prooie. Game continues until all are joined as Prooie.

Special Hints:

Makes sure all keep their eyes closed. If game ends too quickly, expand boundaries.

MJ Jessen

Activity Level 4

Are We Near You?

Activity Level: 4 Age Level: 7+
Location: Ouside Group Size: 6
Materials: Blindfold

Game Description:
Best played on a narrow hiking trail. One child sent ahead on the trail until she is out of sight. She steps off the trail and sits, blindfolded. After she is settled, the leader starts the group walking. They walk slowly, carefully, and as silently as possible. *No talking.* The object of the game is for the group to secretly file past the blindfolded player. When the blindfolded player thinks she hears them she points and says aloud, "I hear you." Upon hearing the words, everyone freezes. The blindfolded child points to where she heard the sound. If she is close to someone, then the game ends and someone takes her place. If she misses, the group keeps moving. The blindfolded player can point three times in a turn.
Variations:
Have the blindfolded child cup her hands behind her ears to amplify sound. Group can file past one by one, or as a unit.
Special Hints:
The blindfolded child can be the prey; a deer, mouse, etc. The group are predators; coyote, hawk, humans, etc. Discuss both roles afterward. Often, the prey has feelings of being hunted. Group frustrations may surface if one or two make a noise which reveals the whole group.

What Animal Am I?

Activity Level: 4 Age Level: 6+
Location: Inside or outside Group Size: 5
Materials: Pictures of animals and safety pins

Game Description:
A picture of a different animal is pinned to each player's back. The player asks yes or no questions of the other players and tries to guess the animal.

Variations:
Substitute environments, buildings or people for animals.

Special Hints:
Start easy and make sure players circulate while asking questions.

Pinocchio

Activity Level: 4 Age Level: 4+
Location: Inside or outside Group Size: 2

Game Description:
One partner is a puppet on the ground, unable to move. The other child is puppeteer and moves the child by pulling imaginary strings.

Special Hints:
Do a few practice turns so children get the feel. Vary partners. Subtle non-verbal communication skills enhanced.

Talking Without Words

Activity Level: 4 Age Level: 4+
Location: Inside or outside Group Size: 2

Game Description:
One player makes nonsense sounds and the partner responds with a movement showing how the sound made her feel. A conversation develops.

Variations:
Do it in larger groups. Bring in props.

Special Hints:
Start with short interactions and let "vocabularies" build in time. Creates a new dimension in communication.

Rhythm Pulse

Activity Level: 4 Age Level: 6+
Location: Inside or outside Group Size: 4

Game Description:
Group sits in a circle with hands joined. One person starts a pattern of squeezes in one direction. This pattern is a pulse. For example: 3 quick squeezes, followed by 2 long squeezes. The pulse is passed around the circle until it is back with the person who started it. Object is to keep the pulse from altering.
Special Hints:
No more than 8 people, so everyone has a chance to start a pulse before tiring of the game. Excellent for quieting and focusing energy. Good at the end of the day. If played with less than 5, use complicated pulses. Short discussion of each pulse can be interesting.

Hit the Nail

Activity Level: 4 Age Level: 4+
Location: Inside or outside Group Size: 4
Materials: Board; hammer; nails

Game Description:
Start a nail in the board. Now each player takes one turn hitting the nail. See how few strokes the class can use to get the nail all the way in.
Variations:
Use the weaker arm. Try blindfolded. Vary nail size or hammer size. Apply the same principle to sawing through wood.
Special Hints:
Watch out for "machos." Make sure no one gets hurt.

Sleeper

Activity Level: 4 Age Level: 7+
Location: Inside or outside Group Size: 10

Game Description:
Players cover eyes. Leader silently chooses Sleeper. Players open eyes and start to mingle. Sleeper puts a player to sleep by winking once at her. Player counts silently to 3 and falls asleep on the floor. Play continues until someone guesses who the Sleeper is.
Variations:
Can be played sitting in a circle.
Special Hints:
Encourage players to look into each other's eyes. No guessing who Sleeper is until at least one person is asleep. Encourage players to be discreet with their winks. One guess per player as to who the Sleeper is.

Two Way Copy

Activity Level: 4 Age Level: 4+
Location: Inside or outside Group Size: 2

Game Description:
First, two children face one another. One moves and the other mirrors her movements. Next, one child stands behind the other. As the first one moves, the following child shadows the movements.
Variations:
Limit to the face. Allow movement in mirrors.
Special Hints:
Good for mixed ages. Older children will enjoy doing this with little ones. Do not let it become competitive. Vary partners.

In Between

Activity Level: 4 Age Level: 3+
Location: Inside or outside Group Size: 2
Materials: Large rubber ball or other objects, depending on variations

Game Description:
Two children face each other and balance a ball between their bodies without using their hands.
Variations:
Increase amount of players. Substitute other objects for the ball. Have players hold a board and balance objects on it. Let them walk around.
Special Hints:
Increase complexity to keep it interesting. Help the little ones. Do it yourself.

Find Your Rock

Activity Level: 4 Age Level: 4+
Location: Outside Group Size: 6
Materials: A cloth to lay rocks on

Game Description:
Each player finds a special rock. Give them 4 minutes to get to know it using all senses. Place rocks on cloth or cleared surface. Group sits around rock pile. With their eyes closed, they try to find their rock by touch. When the believe they have theirs, they open their eyes to see if they are right.
Variations:
Place large cloth over rocks so they can search with eyes open. Add rocks that belong to nobody. Use other natural objects.

Special Hints:
At first, make suggestions as they feel their rocks: Warm? Smooth? Establish size limits so they are encouraged to notice characteristics other than size.

Clothes Switch

Activity Level: 4
Age Level: 5+
Location: Inside or outside
Group Size: 2
Materials: Large old shirt

Game Description:
One player wears a vary large old shirt. Partners hold hands. The aim is to get the shirt onto the second partner without letting go of the hands.
Special Hints:
Help the little ones. Let older ones having conflict try this one together.

I Am

Activity Level: 4
Age Level: 5+
Location: Inside or outside
Group Size: 7

Game Description:
All stand in a circle. Taking turns, each player goes to the middle and calls her name and makes a sound and movement. Then everyone imitates the person in the middle while she watches. Then the next person goes.
Variations:
If the group is close, have one child do another's name. Be an animal instead of yourself.
Special Hints:
Good for warm-up or introductions. Good for group recentering.

Canyon Echo

Activity Level: 4 Age Level: 5+
Location: Outside Group Size: 4

Game Description:
Group is on a trail, single file. First and last in line are the canyon walls. All the players in between are the canyon air that the echo travels through. The head of the line starts the echo. Echo can be any sound or noise pattern. The echo is passed from person to person down the canyon air until it hits the canyon wall, which is the last person in the line. The wall then starts a new and different echo which travels through the air to the head of the line again. After voicing the echo, person 1 steps off the trail and rejoins the line after it files past, becoming the end of the line, or the opposite canyon wall. The new lead person starts a new echo.
Variations:
Introduce a movement to go with the sound.
Special Hints:
Encourage many different sounds. Start game with story about canyons and echoes. Great for children who are getting tired or bored while hiking, for they begin to focus on one another rather than the discomfort. Keeps children from getting separated from the group.

Psychic Nonsense

Activity Level: 4 Age Level: 5+
Location: Inside or outside Group Size: 2

Game Description:
Players decide on three sound and motion movements. One example of a sound and motion movement is flapping

the arms and cawing like a crow. They then turn their backs to one another. On the count of three, they turn around and do one of the three movements. The aim is for everyone to do the same one.

Special Hints:

Join the fun!

Back to Back

Activity Level: 4　　Age Level: 4+

Location: Inside or outside　　Group Size: 2

Game Description:

Two children sit back to back and attempt to get up without using their hands.

Variations:

Vary group size.

Special Hints:

If difficult, suggest they link elbows. Let children in conflict try this together.

Catch Me

Activity Level:4　　Age Level: 7+

Location: Inside or outside　　Group Size: 7

Game Description:

About seven children form a tight circle. One child in the middle stiffens her body and falls in any direction. The others catch her and gently push her around.

Variations:

Vary the rhythm of the passing.

Special Hints:

Make sure the children are attentive. Nice way to start the day.

Chief

Activity Level: 4 Age Level: 4+
Location: Inside or outside Group Size: 8

Game Description:

One player goes where she cannot see the others. A leader is chosen. She does a movement which the others follow. The leader changes the movement regularly. The others follow the leader's movement. The hidden one returns and by watching everyone tries to guess who the leader is.

Variations:

Send more than one away and have them confer. Limit the guesses. Have two leaders and switch off movements. Use movements that make no sound.

Special Hints:

Join the fun!

A What?

Activity Level: 4 Age Level: 7+
Location: Inside or outside Group Size: 8
Materials: Two balls

Game Description:

Players are in a circle. Player 1 hands a ball to Player 2 and says, "this is a banana." Player 2 asks, "a what?" "A banana," says Player 1. "Oh, a banana," says Player 2, who then hands the ball to Player 3 and says "This is a banana." While the "banana" goes around the circle clockwise, the other ball, a "pineapple," goes around the circle counterclockwise, with the same verbal procedures.

Special Hints:

Practice a few times before judging this one. It always turns out to be great fun and a tension breaker. People will play it often to get it right, for it is hard to make both balls go all the way around. Make up silly names for the objects.

Make Me Into You

Activity Level: 4 Age Level: 6+
Location: Inside or outside Group Size: 3

Game Description:
One player closes their eyes. Another forms a sculptured pose. The one with their eyes closed sculpts the third player into the pose chosen by player two, based on sense of touch.
Special Hints:
No one has ever abused this game. Brings out the gentleness in people.

Cast Your Vote

Activity Level: 4 Age Level: 5+
Location: Inside or outside Group Size: 6

Game Description:
Draw a line on the ground that represents a continuum from "strongly agree" to "strongly disagree." Introduce topics and let children vote by where they stand. No talking.
Variations:
Use raising of hands or voice vote.
Special Hints:
Do not vote yourself. Make jokes. Include issues from classroom and family. Great for values clarification as it allows older children to express opinions on sensitive issues.

Subtle Pressure

Activity Level: 4 Age Level: 9+
Location: Inside or outside Group Size: 2

Game Description:
Partners face off. Player one puts their hand on player two's head and slowly presses down. Player two reacts to the pressure by sinking a bit. Then, slowly, player one's hand is lighter and player two feels herself pulled up. Do it a few times and switch roles.
Special Hints:
This is a subtle and sensitive game, best done with people who are caring for one another or who might be caring if given the chance.

Circuits

Activity Level: 4 Age Level: 8+
Location: Inside or outside Group Size: 8

Game Description:
All players in a circle. Pass hand squeezes to the left saying "laa." Pass hand squeezes to the right saying "maa."
Variations:
Add and subtract movements and sounds according to abilities.
Special Hints:
A subtle game of coordination. Can evolve with the children.

Guess Our Shape

Activity Level: 4 Age Level: 4+
Location: In or outside Group Size: 4

Game Description:
Children divide into two groups. One group decides on

a shape to imitate, such as a crocodile or an ice cream cone, using every person in the group. The other group must guess what it is or get close. Then it is the other group's turn.

Special Hints:

Creates a peaceful atmosphere.

Body Ball

Activity Level: 4 Age Level: 4+
Location: Inside or outside Group Size: 2
Materials: Beach ball

Game Description:

Without using hands, partners try to get a beach ball from the ground to their heads.

Variations:

Other size balls. More players.

Special Hints:

A good way to let children who are having difficulty with one another be together.

Alphabet

Activity Level: 4 Age Level: 7+
Location: Inside or outside Group Size: 10

Game Description:

Each player becomes one or more letters of the alphabet, then they have to form words.

Variations:

Time the children. Name a theme. Make a sentence.

Special Hints:

Good for teaching spelling, etc. Can be combined with animal games.

Direct Me

Activity Level: 4 Age Level: 3+
Location: Inside or outside Group Size: 4
Materials: Rock and blindfold

Game Description:
Children stand in a circle, with one in the middle blindfolded. Place the rock on the floor. Circle tries to direct blindfolded player to step on the rock.
Variations:
Vary sophistication of directions allowed. Blindfold partners.
Special Hints:
Good way to teach directions to young children.

Getting Together

Activity Level: 4 Age Level: 5+
Location: Inside Group Size: 15

Game Description:
Count off by ones, twos and threes. Everyone walks around shaking hands with whomever they meet. Ones shake once, twos give two shakes and so on. When they find someone with the same number they hold hands until all of the same numbers are joined.
Special Hints:
A good way to form teams.

Hello

Activity Level: 4 Age Level: 3+
Location: Inside or outside Group Size: 12

Game Description:
Players stand in a circle. Each person attempts to make

eye contact with another. Once contact is established those players change places.

Variations:

Add greetings. Funny things to do or say during switching. Add music. Hand clapping of syllables in name as it is spoken.

Special Hints:

Excellent icebreaker. Make sure everyone is included.

Where Is It?

Activity Level: 4 Age Level: 6+
Location: Inside or outside Group Size: 7
Materials: Pebble

Game Description:

In a circle, with one player in the middle whose eyes are closed. Others pass the pebble. The one in the middle opens eyes and tries to guess who has the stone. Others keep passing it or pretend they are passing it. The pebble must always be in motion. Passes and fakes go on in both directions but always between persons next to one another.

Special Hints:

Encourage good fakery.

Huh?

Activity Level: 4 Age Level: 5+
Location: Inside Group Size: 2

Game Description:

Partners talk together without using words. They have to make up sounds that make no sense to them and carry on a conversation.

Variations:
Make the sounds in rhythm to do group poetry. Act out a theme. Do movement and sounds. Have some children guess what the others are doing.
Special Hints:
One of the best for teaching communication.

Mime Rhyme

Activity Level: 4 Age Level: 8+
Location: Inside Group Size: 4+

Game Description:
Player thinks up a word and tells others a word that rhymes with it. Others try to guess the word, but must act out their guess in pantomime. Player tells whether that guess is right.
Special Hints:
Good for new groups, for rainy days and for improving communication.

Human Puzzles

Activity Level: 4 Age Level: 4+
Location: Inside Group Size: 5
Materials: Homemade puzzle pieces

Game Description:
In groups of 5 to 7, each child is given a piece of a puzzle. Working together, they put the puzzle together.
Variations:
Increase complexity. Let group puzzles fit together to make one large puzzle. Let each group make up a story about their puzzle. Let each story be a chapter in the class story puzzle.

Chalkboard Drawing

Activity Level: 4 Age Level: 4+
Location: Inside Group Size: 15
Materials: Chalk and chalkboard

Game Description:
Children draw circles on chalkboard under various handicaps, for instance in opposite direction with each hand; blindfolded; with objects on the back of the hand.
Variations:
Change shapes. Change drawing tool (e.g., chalk held in a clothespin). Work a theme.
Special Hints:
Keep the focus on well-drawn shapes. Helps individuals reentering.

Feel and Find Boxes

Activity Level: 4 Age Level: 5+
Location: Inside Group Size: 1
Materials: Anything and everything

Game Description:
A box is constructed with a curtain on the front. Various objects are placed in it which the children try to guess by touch.
Variations:
Change box size. Change objects. Place duplicates on top for matching. Use objects from nature.
Special Hints:
Increase complexity continually.

MJ Jessen

Activity Level 5

Watch My Face

Activity Level: 5 Age Level: 4+
Location: Inside or outside Group Size: 8

Game Description:
Players stand in a circle. One player starts a crazy face one way. When that one is going she starts another one going the other way. When it makes the round someone else begins.
Variations:
Add a sound.

Try not to Laugh

Activity Level: 5 A ge Level: 4+
Location: Inside or outside Group Size: 4

Game Description:
Players sit in a circle. One is It, and calls "Muk." This ends all conversation and smiling. It is now up to the one who is It to make another talk or smile. Anything goes, but no touching and no averting eyes.
Special Hints:
Play along. Introduce surprise. A good way to calm things down.

What Did I Do?

Activity Level: 5 Age Level: 6+
Location: Inside or outside Group Size: 2

Game Description:
Partners face off. Player A examines player B for a minute or two and then turns her back. Player B changes five things about her appearance. Player A turns around and tries to guess what has been changed.

Variations:
Vary the time of observation and the amount of things changed. Do it with an area and not a person.
Special Hints:
Help out those who get stumped. Don't let it become competitive.

Where Did it Go?

Activity Level: 5 Age Level: 5+
Location: Inside Group Size: 6
Materials: Small bell

Game Description:
One player sits in the middle, blindfolded. The other players pass a bell around with each player ringing it once. They stop and the last one puts it behind her back. The one in the center tries to guess where it is.

Webs

Activity Level: 5 Age Level: 5+
Location: Inside or outside Group Size: 5
Materials: Ball of yarn

Game Description:
Using a big ball of yarn, hold the end and toss the ball to another. All are seated in a circle. The player with the yarn gets to speak to the group. The ball is passed, the end is held, the web is formed.
Variations:
Introduce a theme on which all have to speak.
Special Hints:
Allow the option to pass without speaking. Play fairly regularly for group solidarity. Let important issues arise.

Nature Web

Activity Level: 5
Location: Inside or outside
Materials: Ball of yarn

Age Level: 8+
Group Size: 5

Game Description:

Holding a ball of yarn the leader asks the first child to name a plant. The ball of yarn is thrown to player 1. Then ask: "What animal eats that plant?" The ball is thrown to the second player, 2, with player 1 holding the end. Then ask "What animal eats that animal?" The yarn is thrown to player 3. Then: "Where does that animal live?" and so on until a web representing the local ecology is formed. Then introduce a plausible disaster. Tug on the point of the web that represented that part of the environment that would be destroyed. Who else feels the tug? And so on.

Special Hints:

Here's safe space for everyone to communicate their values concerning the environment.

Dictionary

Activity Level: 5 Age Level: 10
Location: Inside Group Size: 5
Materials: Dictionary; pencils; paper

Game Description:
One player picks a strange word from the dictionary. She writes it down on a slip of paper. She says the word. Everyone else writes down a definition for the word. Then the definitions are read aloud and everyone tries to guess which one was right.
Variations:
Try to guess who wrote which definition.
Special Hints:
Great for vocabulary building. Can be great fun for leaders.

T-Shirts

Activity Level: 5 Age Level: 4+
Location: Inside Group Size: 6
Materials: T-shirt outline on a piece of paper; scissors; drawing tools

Game Description:
Give each child a piece of paper with a T-shirt outline on it. Let them cut the shirt out and write their name in the middle. Then ask them questions about their life and values and have them write or draw the answers on various parts of the shirt.
Variations:
Examples: favorite animal, place in home, or memory.
Special Hints:
Allow time for decorating. Excellent for insight into values. Builds self-esteem.

ReConnect

Activity Level: 5 | Age Level: 5+
Location: Inside or outside | Group Size: 2

Game Description:
Eyes closed, partners face off, touch palms, feel the energy and drop arms. Then take two steps back, turn three times and try to reconnect palms.

Variations:
Bend arms and try to touch agreed upon other body parts. Do it in a circle.

Special Hints:
It's fun to watch, so make it a group activity even if only two are playing.

Guess

Activity Level: 5 | Age Level: 4+
Location: Inside | Group Size: 5+
Materials: Weird handheld objects and a sheet

Game Description:
Players sit in a circle with sheet covering hands and lower arms. Weird object is passed around under the sheet and everyone tries to guess what it is.

Variations:
Choose object suitable to level of players.

Special Hints:
Let little ones feel first before guessing. Guess in turn and don't reveal until the end. Or, guess silently so no one feels left out.

Casual Conversation

Activity Level: 5 | Age Level: 8+
Location: Inside or outside | Group Size: 6

Game Description:

The group sends two people out of earshot and decides on two different sentences. The pair is called back and each is privately told one of the sentences. The pair proceed to have a "conversation." Each tries to insert their sentence into the conversation before the other. If the other speaker suspects the sentence has been said, she can challenge. Each player is allowed three challenges. When the sentence is either challenged correctely or passes undetected, the game is over and two new players go.

Special Hints:

Younger children will need some coaching at first. Remind them to develop conversation before attempting to insert their sentence. Sample sentences: "When salmon spawn they turn bright red." Or "Human beings have 40 million brain cells." Good game to pair children who don't often talk to each other or play together. With care, it serves to pair children who don't get along.

Silent Drawing

Activity Level: 5 Age Level: 4+
Location: Inside Group Size: 2
Materials: Drawing tools; painting tools; large sheets of paper

Game Description:

Two players hold the same brush or crayon and draw on the same piece of paper. No talking.

Variations:

Have several pairs draw on the same piece of paper. Let one pair finish before the next begins. Suggest a theme.

Special Hints:

Vary partners. Encourage slow starters.

Do You Know Me?

Activity Level: 5 Age Level: 4+
Location: Inside or outside Group Size: 8
Materials: Blindfold

Game Description:
A blindfolded player is led to the group sitting in a line or semicircle. She is told to identify one person in the group by gently touching everyone's face, one by one, until she finds who she is looking for. After she guesses, the blindfold is removed and another player goes.
Variations:
Identification by touching hands only. Identify each person as they are touched.
Special Hints:
Only touch face, not clothing or jewelry. Silence is critical.

Silent Structures

Activity Level: 5 Age Level: 6+
Location: Inside Group Size: 4
Materials: Colored paper; masking tape; scissors

Game Description:
Divide children into groups of 4 to 6. Give each group two pairs of scissors, two rolls of masking tape and a stack of colored paper. One color per group. Tell the children to build a castle. No talking allowed.
Variations:
Allow talking. Use random materials at hand.
Special Hints:
Hold a discussion afterwards to bring out decision-making role of each child. Vary group makeup. Builds nonverbal communication skills.

Cooperative House Play

Activity Level: 5 Age Level: 3+
Location: Inside or outside Group Size: 2
Materials: Varies

Game Description:
Work around the house can be turned into a cooperative adventure. Cooking can be done with only one hand, or with only one person knowing the recipe and no talking allowed. Gardening can also be done under similar handicaps to promote cooperation.
Variations:
Limited only by your imagination.
Special Hints:
Approach with good humor and no time limit.

Lion, Fox, Deer, Dove

Activity Level: 5 Age Level: 7+
Location: Inside Group Size: 12
Materials: Four pieces of poster board and a marker

Game Description:
Make a poster board sign each for Lion, Fox, Deer and Dove. Ask the players to go to the animal that they most resemble and join the group. Let them discuss among themselves why they picked that animal. Then a spokesperson from each group explains to everyone the feelings and thoughts of her animal group.
Variations:
Pick other animals or issues to discuss.
Special Hints:
The discussion is critical. It will reveal the predispositions of the players.

Prehistoric Communication

Activity Level: 5 Age Level: 8+
Location: Inside Group Size: 4
Materials: Paper and drawing tools

Game Description:
Form groups of 4. One from each group comes to the leader, who whispers a word in her ear. That person turns to the group and draws the word or phrase while the others try to guess. Then another player gets a new word.
Variations:
Two do the drawing holding one drawing tool, either communicating with one another or not. Can draw more than one picture.
Special Hints:
If it goes too long, the next person goes.

Cooperative Storytelling

Activity Level: 5 Age Level: 3+
Location: Inside or outside Group Size: 3

Game Description:
Players make up a story one sentence at a time, with each player taking a turn.
Variations:
Each player takes a paragraph. Introduce a theme. Leader takes the lead and keeps the theme alive.
Special Hints:
Encourage all to play. Excellent around a campfire. Can lead to collective picture.

Collage

Activity Level: 5 Age Level: 5+
Location: Inside Group Size: 4
Materials: Glue; scissors; old magazines; poster board

Game Description:
A theme is introduced and the group collectively creates a collage.
Variations:
Any theme. Can make a group gift.
Special Hints:
Good for a rainy day.

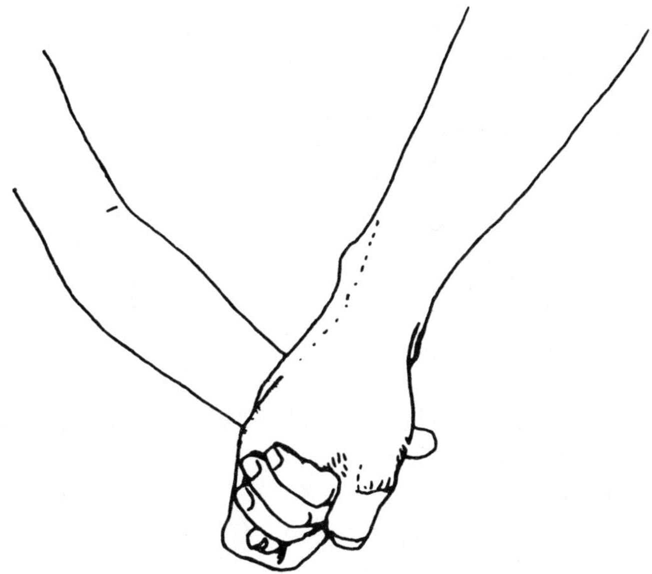

Books About Cooperative Games

Cain, Jim and Barry Jolliff. *Teamwork & Teamplay.* Kendall/Hunt Publishing, 1998.

Cain, Jim and Tom Smith. *The Book on Raccoon Circles.* Learning Unlimited, 2002.

Gibbs, Jeanne. *Tribes: A New Way of Learning and Being Together.* Centersource Systems, 2001.

Lefevre, Dale N. *Best New Games: 77 Games and 7 Trust Activities for All Ages and Abilities.* Human Kinetics Publishers, 2001.

Luvmour, Sambhava and Josette Luvmour. *Win-Win Games for All Ages: Cooperative Activities for Building Social Skills.* New Society Publishers, 2002.

Rohnke, Karl E. *Silver Bullets: A Guide to Initiative Problems, Adventure Games and Trust Activities.* Kendall/Hunt Publishing, 1989. (Reprint edition)

Rohnke, Karl E. *Cowstails and Cobras: A Guide to Games, Initiatives, Ropes Courses and Adventure Curriculum.* Kendall/Hunt Publishing, 2003.

Sikes, Sam. *Raptor.* Kendall/Hunt Publishing, 1998.

Indices

Games Group Size Index

One or more players

Two or More Players

Three or More Players

Four or More Players

Five or More Players

Six or More Players

Seven or More Players

Eight or More Players

Games Age Level Index

Age One and Up

Age Three and Up

Age Four and Up

Age Five and Up

Age Six and Up

Age Seven and Up

Age Eight and Up

Age Nine and Up

About the Authors

Josette and Ba created and developed Natural Learning Rhythms (NLR) – a whole-child understanding of Child Development that supports optimal well-being in children. They have been using NLR with children, families, educators, and therapists for over twenty-five years. Educators, consultants, and seminar leaders, Josette and Ba are advisors to public and private schools as well as authors specializing in whole-child development, education, and family dynamics.

They are originators and Directors of EnCompass, originally founded as Center for Educational Guidance twenty-two years ago. NLR is the basis and philosophical foundation for all EnCompass programs.

If we can be of any help to you, please do not hesitate to write.

Ba Luvmour, Josette Luvmour
EnCompass
4133 NE 30th Avenue
Portland, OR 97211
(503) 287-1785
EnCompassFamilies.org

If you have enjoyed *Everyone Wins* you might also enjoy other

BOOKS TO BUILD A NEW SOCIETY

Our books provide positive solutions for people
who want to make a difference. We specialize in:

Environment and Justice • Conscientious Commerce
Sustainable Living • Ecological Design and Planning
Natural Building & Appropriate Technology
Educational and Parenting Resources • Nonviolence
Progressive Leadership • Resistance and Community

New Society Publishers

ENVIRONMENTAL BENEFITS STATEMENT

New Society Publishers has chosen to produce this book on Enviro 100, recycled paper made with **100% post consumer waste**, processed chlorine free, and old growth free.

For every 5,000 books printed, New Society saves the following resources:[1]

17	Trees
1,536	Pounds of Solid Waste
1,691	Gallons of Water
2,205	Kilowatt Hours of Electricity
2,793	Pounds of Greenhouse Gases
12	Pounds of HAPs, VOCs, and AOX Combined
4	Cubic Yards of Landfill Space

[1]Environmental benefits are calculated based on research done by the Environmental Defense Fund and other members of the Paper Task Force who study the environmental impacts of the paper industry.

For more information on this environmental benefits statement, or to inquire about environmentally friendly papers, please contact New Leaf Paper – info@newleafpaper.com Tel: 888 • 989 • 5323.

For a full list of NSP's titles, please call **1-800-567-6772**
or check out our website at:

www.newsociety.com

NEW SOCIETY PUBLISHERS

Our books provide positive solutions for people who want to make a difference.

For a copy of our catalog, please mail this card to us.

We specialize in the following; please indicate your area/s of interest:

❑ Activism
❑ Globalization
❑ Ecological Design & Planning
❑ Environment & Economy
❑ Conscientious Commerce
❑ Sustainable Living
❑ Environmental Education
❑ Education & Parenting
❑ Progressive Leadership
❑ Conflict Education
❑ Storytelling
❑ Natural Building & Renewable Energy
❑ Making a Difference

❑ *Please subscribe me to* New Society News — *our monthly e-mail newsletter.*

Name______________________________

Address/City/Province______________________________

Postal Code/Zip_______________ Email Address_______________

toll-free 800-567-6772 **www.newsociety.com**

NEW SOCIETY PUBLISHERS

Our books provide positive solutions for people who want to make a difference.

For a copy of our catalog, please mail this card to us.

We specialize in the following; please indicate your area/s of interest:

❑ Activism
❑ Globalization
❑ Ecological Design & Planning
❑ Environment & Economy
❑ Conscientious Commerce
❑ Sustainable Living
❑ Environmental Education
❑ Education & Parenting
❑ Progressive Leadership
❑ Conflict Education
❑ Storytelling
❑ Natural Building & Renewable Energy
❑ Making a Difference

❑ *Please subscribe me to* New Society News — *our monthly e-mail newsletter.*

Name______________________________

Address/City/Province______________________________

Postal Code/Zip_______________ Email Address_______________

toll-free 800-567-6772  **www.newsociety.com**

NEW SOCIETY PUBLISHERS

Place
Postage
Here

NEW SOCIETY PUBLISHERS
P.O. Box 189
Gabriola Island,
B.C. V0R 1X0
Canada

BOOKS TO BUILD A NEW SOCIETY

Place
Postage
Here

NEW SOCIETY PUBLISHERS
P.O. Box 189
Gabriola Island,
B.C. V0R 1X0
Canada

BOOKS TO BUILD A NEW SOCIETY